MW01539724

Do Not Give Up Your Gummy Bears to Borrow a Teddy Bear:

Just Say NO to Debt

by

Chanise Okonkwo

Illustrated by

Diego Barbosa

Do Not Give Up Your Gummy Bears to Borrow a Teddy Bear:
Just Say NO to Debt

Copyright © 2019 by Chanise Okonkwo.

All rights reserved.

No part of this book may be reproduced, distributed, stored in a retrieval system, or transmitted in any form or by any means, electronic, mechanical, photocopying, recording, or otherwise, without the prior written permission of the author.

Contact me: chanise78@gmail.com

Front cover design: Diego Barbosa

Printed in the United States of America

For Jacob, Jayden, & Jenesis

May you achieve abundance of success in life
and your hearts desires come true

Jacob and Jayden were playing basketball when Jacob stopped.

"Listen," he said.

"Whoopee!"

"Hooray!"

"Yippee!"

Jayden looked puzzled. "Why are Mom and Dad shouting?"

The boys ran into the living room.

"Mom! Dad! What's going on?" Jacob asked.

"Yeah," Jayden said, looking around. "We heard you guys shouting. What's happening?"

"We finally got the huge monkey off our backs," Dad said with a big smile.

"What!" Jayden exclaimed. "We have a monkey? Where?"

"No, silly, we don't have a monkey. Get the monkey off your back is a figure of speech," Mom explained. "What your dad is saying is that we accomplished something that's been bugging us for years."

"That's right. Your mom and I finished paying off all our debt," Dad said.

"We're celebrating because we're debt free."

"Oh. Okay," said Jacob. Jayden shrugged.

"Whatever you do, don't get into debt. Just say no to debt!" said Dad.

"Okay, Dad, but what is debt?" asked Jacob.

"Yeah, what is debt?" said Jayden.

"Debt is what you owe because you borrowed something. I don't want either of you to get into debt with money. When you borrow money, you have to pay back the money you borrowed plus more money called interest. So if you borrow $100 dollars, you have to pay back the $100 plus the interest."

Jacob and Jayden did not understand what the big deal was, but they said, "Don't worry, Dad. We won't get into debt."

The next day at school after lunch Jayden was getting ready for nap time. He went to his cubby to get his blanket and Yogi, his teddy bear, only—Yogi was not there. Oh, no! I forgot Yogi at home. What am I going to do? Jayden could not sleep at naptime without Yogi. Three cubbies away, he saw that his friend José had two teddy bears.

"José, may I please borrow one of your teddy bears?" Jayden asked.
"Sure," said José, "but only if you promise to give me your gummy bears
from your lunch box every day for five days— starting next week."
Jayden loved gummy bears, but he really, really wanted a teddy bear now!
"Okay," he agreed. They shook hands to seal the deal.

The teddy bear had big brown eyes that seemed to smile at Jayden. It was so soft, so fluffy, and just the right size to snuggle with that Jayden fell asleep right away. Jayden liked taking a nap with José's teddy bear. In fact, he liked it so much that he asked José if he could borrow the teddy bear again the next day.

"Sure," said José, "but you'll have to give me your gummy bears for five more days. Five days next week and five days the following week will make ten days all together."

Hmmm, Jayden thought. I already have to give him my gummy bears for five days for borrowing his teddy bear yesterday. Another five days won't be that bad. "Okay, I'll do it," he said. They shook hands to seal the deal.

Jayden really, really, really liked Jose's teddy bear. In fact, he liked that teddy bear so much that he borrowed it for a third day and a fourth day! Each time José add another five days to the days that Jayden had to give him his gummy bears.

On Monday, Day 1, Jayden took the gummy bears from his lunch and gave them to José as promised.

On Tuesday, Day 2, Jayden gave José his gummy bears.

On Wednesday, Day 3, Jayden gave José his gummy bears, but Jayden was sad. He wanted to eat his gummy bears, but he had agreed to give them to José for borrowing his teddy bear. On Thursday, Day 4, Jayden gave José his gummy bears.

On Friday, Day 5, Jayden opened his lunch box to give José his gummy bears and saw— sour blue raspberry, his favorite! Bummer, Jayden thought. I want to eat my gummy bears, but I can't because I borrowed José's teddy bear four times!

Each time I borrowed the bear, I promised to give José my gummy bears for five days, so let me see: I owe 5 . . . 10 . . . 15 . . . 20— Oh, no! Twenty days of no gummies?

Twenty days of no wiggly, jiggly fun worm gummies? Twenty days of no cherry, lemon, or watermelon flavored gummies—or my favorite, sour blue-raspberry gummies? And today is only Day 5? NNNOOOOO!

That evening, while they were eating dinner, Jayden's mother noticed his shoulders were slumped and that he was picking at his food and frowning. "What's wrong, Jayden?" she asked.

"Yeah, kiddo, you didn't even want to play basketball with Jacob and me," said Dad.

Jayden told his parents about having borrowed José's teddy bear and now having to give him his gummy bears. "I wish I'd never borrowed his teddy bear at all. By the time I'm done giving José my gummies, I'll forget what they taste like. I'll be so old by then that I won't be able to eat gummies at all because I won't have any teeth. I'll never taste gummies again!"

"I'm sure, Jayden," Mom said, "that you'll still remember what gummies taste like after you're done paying your debt, and you will still have your teeth, silly."

"Paying my what?" asked Jayden.

"Your debt," said his mom.

"Remember a week ago when I told you guys not to get into debt?" their dad asked.

"Yes," said Jacob and Jayden together. "But I really didn't get what you were talking about, Dad," Jayden said.

"Neither did I," said Jacob.

"Well, borrowing José's teddy bear is like borrowing money," Dad explained.

"And Jayden's having to give José his gummies is the interest he had to pay for borrowing the teddy bear?" Jacob said.

Dad nodded. "Correct!"

"So when I borrow something," Jayden said, "I always have to give it back because it's not mine. I have to give it back—plus interest."

"You got it, kiddo" said their dad.

"Oh, now I get why you're so happy to be done paying off all your debt," said Jacob.

"Yeah, I get it, too! And I'm glad you get to enjoy your gummies—I mean money—again. When I'm done paying off my debt, I'm going to shout yippee, jump up and down, and, best of all, eat my gummy bears! But right now, please excuse me. I need to go do something really quick."

Jayden jumped up from the table and started toward his room.

"What is it?" his mom asked.

"I'm going to make sure Yogi is in my backpack. I'm not owing anybody any more gummies. From now on, I'm saying NO to debt."

Made in the USA
Las Vegas, NV
05 March 2023

68548346R00017